Pebble® Plus

HOW GARBAGE GETS FROM TRASH CANS TO LANDFILLS

by Erika L. Shores

Consultant: George Dreckmann
Strategic Initiatives Coordinator
City of Madison (Wisconsin) Streets Division

CAPSTONE PRESS
a capstone imprint

Pebble Plus is published by Capstone Press,
1710 Roe Crest Drive, North Mankato, Minnesota 56003
www.mycapstone.com

Library of Congress Cataloging-in-Publication Data
Cataloging-in-publication information is on file with the Library of Congress.
ISBN 978-1-4914-8433-3 (library binding)
ISBN 978-1-4914-8437-1 (paperback)
ISBN 978-1-4914-8441-8 (eBook PDF)

Editorial Credits
Jill Kalz, editor; Juliette Peters and Katelin Plekkenpol, designers;
Morgan Walters, media researcher; Laura Manthe, production specialist

Photo Credits
Dreamstime: Franco Ricci, 15, Mauricio Jordan De Souza Coelho, 20; George P. Dreckmann,
11; Shutterstock: Awe Inspiring Images, 19, bikeriderlondon, 17, dogi, 8, GongTo, 3, Hurst
Photo, 9, hxdyl, (bottom) cover, Ivan Cholakov, 10, jajaladdawan, (top left) cover, Joseph Sohm,
18, kanvag, 12, KieferPix, 21, NRT, 6, nw10photography, 7, Paul Vasarhelyi, 16, Peter Gudella,
5, photka, (top right) cover, photka, 22-23, Ulrich Mueller, 14, WitthayaP, back cover, 1, Yuriy
Chertok, 13

Printed in the United States of America in North Mankato, Minnesota.
052016 009754R

Note to Parents and Teachers

The Here to There set supports national curriculum standards for science and social studies
related to technology and the roles of community workers. This book describes and illustrates
the journey waste takes from cans and bins to landfills and recycling centers. The images
support early readers in understanding the text. The repetition of words and phrases helps
early readers in understanding the text. This book also introduces early readers to subject-
specific vocabulary words, which are defined in the Glossary section. Early readers may need
assistance to read some words and to use the Table of Contents, Glossary, Read More, Internet
Sites, Critical Thinking Using the Common Core, and Index sections of the book.

TABLE OF CONTENTS

Take Out the Garbage

Every day we throw away

food and drink containers,

bottles, and paper.

Where does this garbage go?

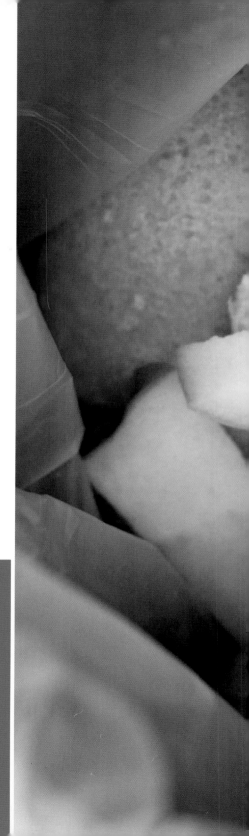

Garbage is also called waste.

Waste is anything that

is no longer used.

Everything from old food

to broken toys can be waste.

People toss waste into
garbage cans and recycling bins.
The waste in recycling bins
will be made into new things.

Buried or Burned

Here comes the garbage truck!

A special arm grabs the can.

It dumps the can's garbage

into the truck.

arm

Garbage collectors haul waste
from homes and businesses
to a landfill. Workers there
pile up the waste and bury it.

Sometimes waste is burned
instead of buried.
Heat from burning waste
makes steam. The steam can be
used to make electricity.

Waste is collected for burning.

Used to New

Waste in recycling bins

does not go to a landfill.

A recycling truck collects it

and takes it to a recycling center.

Workers sort plastics,

papers, metals, and glass

into giant bundles.

Companies buy the materials.

They turn them into new products.

Making Less Waste

You can make less waste.

Buy only what you need.

Use your own cloth bags at stores.

Buy a water bottle to use

over and over again.

GLOSSARY

electricity—a natural force that can be used to make light and heat or to make machines work

landfill—a place where garbage is buried

material—the matter from which a thing is or can be made

recycle—to make used items into new products; people can recycle items such as rubber, glass, plastic, and aluminum

steam—the gas that water turns into when it boils

waste—anything that is no longer needed or used; waste is another word for garbage or trash

READ MORE

Alexander, Richard. *What Do Garbage Collectors Do?* Helping the Community. New York: PowerKids Press, 2016.

Lawrence, Ellen. *Garbage Galore.* Green World, Clean World. New York: Bearport Publishing, 2014.

Pettiford, Rebecca. *Garbage Collectors.* Community Helpers. Minneapolis: Jump!, 2015.

INTERNET SITES

FactHound offers a safe, fun way to find Internet sites related to this book. All of the sites on FactHound have been researched by our staff.

Here's all you do:

Visit *www.facthound.com*

Type in this code: 9781491484333

Super-cool stuff!

Check out projects, games and lots more at
www.capstonekids.com

CRITICAL THINKING USING THE COMMON CORE

1. Use the text and photographs on pages 12 to 15 to describe a landfill. (Key Ideas and Details)

2. Why is it important to make less waste? (Integration of Knowledge and Ideas)

INDEX